James Cook

Thea Stanley Hughes

LIST OF ILLUSTRATIONS

ISBN 0 908076 13 4

Copyright © Movement Publications 1981

Second   Impression — 1981
Third   Impression — 1982
Fourth   Impression — 1986
Fifth   Impression — 1988
Sixth   Impression — 1990
Seventh Impression — 1992
Eighth   Impression — 1995

Typeset by Frontier Technology Pty Limited
66 Spit Road, Spit Junction, NSW 2088

Printed in Australia by Star Printery Pty. Limited
21 Coulson Street, Erskineville, NSW 2043

Contents

We are all blind, until we see
That in the human plan
Nothing is worth the making if
It does not make the man.

Why build these cities glorious
If man unbuilded goes?
In vain we build the work, unless
The builder also grows.

Edwin Markham.

"The man who does not restrain wantonness allies himself with beasts. It is easier to contend with evil at the beginning than at the end. You can have no greater and no smaller dominion than that over yourself."

Leonardo da Vinci.

Introduction

Australia is a very interesting continent. It was the last land mass to be discovered, though it is one of the very oldest parts of the earth. It is closer in space to the eastern peoples, though it has the same sort of culture as the western peoples. It has many different climates and there are plants and animals on it that do not make their homes anywhere else and hovering above it always is a group of stars that are not in the northern skies.

It was to the sun and stars that the early navigators looked for help for knowing where they were and for plotting the course decided by the captain. When men sailed from the northern to the southern oceans, they noticed something they had never seen before. To them, it was a new shape among the stars — the shape of a cross — that stood out from the other constellations because of its size, brilliance and simplicity. They must soon have noticed that, though the cross moves, the long arm, which ends in the brightest star, always points in a southerly direction. For people who come from other parts of the world to live in Australia, this constellation, the Southern Cross, could be pointing to really new opportunities.

In the year 1768, there was one ship that was under the command of a very great Captain — James Cook. This little ship, with a crew of ninety-four, set out from Britain. Two years later, it reached the Great Southern Land, which had been lying undiscovered in the Pacific Ocean for hundreds of centuries and a landing was made. It was from this moment that it became connected with the life of the British people and, so, with the western world. This land is Australia. To discover it meant not only to be near, to set eyes on or even to set foot on but to locate it and determine the position in such a way that others could find it.

Some people only know that Cook discovered Australia. Others know that he did important work on the west coasts of Canada and North America and on the whole coastline of New Zealand. Still others know about all that and also know that his exploring spirit took him on long east-west and north-south voyages and that he even penetrated both the Arctic and Antarctic Circles, travelling farther south than anybody before. So, we can come to know that he not only discovered Australia for Britain but that, by his life, he linked these countries to each other and also to the world.

Now, from *what* he did we can learn about his endurance capacity and so on. This does not tell us the most important thing and that is what he was like as a man, what his thoughts were like and how much control he had over his feeling, thoughts and actions. However, we can tell something about these important things by knowing something of the *way* he did things, by knowing *what* he did and by knowing *what* he did *not* do and by what his relationship with other people was like. From what he did not do, we can learn the degree of self-mastery he exercised, whether he worried about what other people thought of him or whether he just did what he thought was right for him to do.

James Cook by J.C. Beaglehole, which gives in great detail the story of this very dramatic life, and *The Seamen's Seaman* by Alan Villiers, which gives wonderful descriptions based on Villiers' exceptional experiences, are the two works I have found the most valuable in the production of this small book.

The stimulus for the production of this little book and some helpful advice came from within the circle of the National Parks and Wildlife Service. It is also encouraging to know that the Rangers looking after the landing place and museum at Kurnell have such keen interest in the place and in the children visiting it. This is an attempt to tell part of the story in such a way that those who read it thoughtfully may get some feeling for what this explorer was like as a man.

On account of his many discoveries, Captain Cook belongs to the past. On account of his character, he belongs to the present and to the future. Some who read this book may be able to decide whether he can help us now. To me, it seems that those who are looking after the wildlife of Australia would not have such a difficult and disheartening task if large numbers of people could take an interest, in a practical way, in the life of this man. To achieve this in a practical way means to get to know him and take him as an example.

Taking him as an example would stimulate any wide-awake person to work towards developing those human qualities that are needed for coping with the difficult times ahead and it would help us to have the strength to save what we can save of what is left of our heritage.

In the case of any person ahead of his time, it is the responsibility of those who come after to see to it that the influence does not end with those who knew the individual personally. It is the responsibility of those who come after to see to it that the influence of his life is carried forward into the future.

One question is whether we are big enough to take this life as an example ourselves. Another question is whether we are energetic enough to help others to get to know him.

T.S.H.

CAPTAIN JAMES COOK, F.R.S.

The trust we placed in him was untiring. Our admiration of his great abilities unlimited. Our esteem for his good qualities affectionate and sincere.

David Samwell
Surgeon's Mate (Third Voyage)

JAMES COOK

When a plant appears above the ground, anybody who has studied plants knows what it will be like when it is fully grown and knows what effect it will have on the environment, for instance, whether it will be poisonous or health-giving to animal and man. When an animal is born, anybody who has studied animals knows what it will be like when it is fully grown, what sort of habits can be expected of it, what it will not be able to do and what environment it will have to have. When a human being is born, nobody — not even those who have studied man — knows what he or she will be like in character or habits when grown up or what will be the result of that human being having been born into the world.

CHILDHOOD

When it came to the year 1728 and then to the day of 27th October, James Cook was born into the small farming village of Marton in Yorkshire, England.

Nobody knew that this child would change the map of the world and be called, by some, the greatest seaman-explorer and, by others, the greatest navigator of all times.

Nobody knew that he would spend practically the whole of his life on the sea with men — not with a few chosen friends but with a lot of men — crowded into small quarters for

9

months and sometimes for years at a time with intervals in many new environments. We can have no idea of what this entailed unless we realize that, in all such groups of men, there were some who were good at their jobs and some who were not, there were some who were good at taking orders and some who were not and there were some who wanted to be in that situation and some who did not even want to be at sea at all.

Nobody knew that, when he grew up, he would be very different from the majority of men in abilities, habits and in his effect on many people and environments.

THE COTTAGE WHERE JAMES COOK WAS BORN

James' father was very poor and worked for a farmer. This farmer, noticing unusual abilities in Cook's son, sent the boy, at his own expense, to the school at the nearby village of

Great Ayton. There, from the age of eight, he learnt reading writing and arithmetic. During these years he went on working with his father. Even when he was at school, his relationship with his school mates showed that he had unusual independence and strength of will. Though this sometimes separated him from the majority, he had something about him that made other boys feel deep respect for him.

FIRST JOB

At the age of sixteen, his love of mathematics brought him, first of all, a job in a grocery and draper's shop in the Yorkshire village of Staithes. Now, Staithes was a fishing village and only about thirty-two kilometres (twenty miles) from the busy seaport of Whitby. It is easy for us now to see how important it was for him to get a job in Staithes. The shop was almost on the sea. So, there he was with the sight, the smell and the sound of the sea with him all day long while he attended to the wants of the village people and to the storekeeper's books. It did not take him long to find out that he was greatly attracted to the sea. After hours would find him amongst the fishermen, learning all that can only be learnt from the men of the sea. He would also have heard of the dangers of sailing the North Sea in all her different moods.

The storekeeper soon saw that James was more interested in a life on the sea and, when the boy had stuck to his job for eighteen months, he himself relieved him of it and actually took him to Whitby to introduce him to a Mr. John Walker. The job in the shop was important because it led him to the sea and because the storekeeper was to lead him to Whitby.

So, with the help of his father's employer, he had been given the chance to go to school where his mathematical talent was brought out and then, with the help of his first employer, he had been able to get from the land to the sea

11

without running away from the job in the shop and without even having to ask to be relieved of it. The timing of things is specially significant when the life-work is both difficult and important and it is interesting to see the way in which his path was shown to him, though he was willing to do the work at hand — whatever it was.

WHITBY

Whitby harbour is situated at the mouth of the River Esk in Yorkshire on the east coast of England. With no land between Spitsbergen (an archipelago in the Arctic Circle belonging to Norway) and the Yorkshire coast, a storm-driven sea has time to build up into a fury before it breaks on the coast. The ships have always been in great danger there, because the sea can change from calm to fury so quickly and because of the structure of the coastline. Whitby has a long history of commerce and ship-building going back to the sixteenth century.

APPRENTICESHIP

John Walker was a Quaker, a well-known ship owner and trader with premises at Grape Lane, Whitby — which are still there. James became apprenticed to him for three years. It was not long before his employer became aware of his ability and sent him to sea at once but, in the winter months, he kept him at home to study mathematics and navigation. It is said that James worked by the light of a candle long into the night in the low-rafted attic at the top of the house.

It must be remembered that, at this time, there were no trains or big trucks and most of the carrying was done by ships. In the north of England there was much mining for coal and about one million tonnes of it were shipped to London each year. To do this, there were about 400 small ships that made about four journeys a year if the weather permitted.

WHITBY HARBOUR — about the time of Captain Cook

THE ATTIC ROOM, GRAPE LANE, WHITBY, WHERE JAMES COOK STUDIED

It must also be remembered that, in those days, the charting of the treacherous coast was not accurate and that there were no lights and buoys to mark out the danger spots. All these danger spots had to be learnt. It took courage to do the coast run or to take part in the trade between England and the Continent. These waters were well named 'a nursery of seamen'. Those who survived their time would have been well equipped but many died.

During the boy's apprenticeship, Walker had a new ship built and James was given the job of helping with the fitting and rigging. This gave him the chance to learn the sails and rigging very thoroughly.

As there were so many apprentices at this time, not much was recorded of the individual but we can gather that it was the sort of training that stood the boy in good stead for his future work.

MERCHANT NAVY

When he had served his time with Mr. Walker, James spent two years before the mast in the Baltic trade. He then returned, with the rank of Mate, to Walker and worked for him for the next three years. On the River Thames he showed great ability in manoeuvring a craft entirely dependent on sail on a crowded waterway, often against the dictates of the wind and tide. This did not go unnoticed and he was moved to the North Sea run on which, in all weathers, the ships sailed up the Baltic Sea and on to Norway. The ship that he was on at this time, a barque — that is a vessel with three sails and no mizzen topsail — weighed only 465 tonnes. He was to gain confidence in the barque's durability and seaworthiness — a confidence that was fully justified.

Due to his skill and the build of the ship he got safely through many a violent storm. During one voyage, out of fifteen ships, only six survived a tremendous gale to creep back to their home port with all that remained of their crews utterly exhausted and suffering dreadfully from the effects of the relentless effort to survive and the exposure to the raging elements. By the time they made the safety of their harbour the poor ships were leaking like sieves and their decks had been swept clear of all gear by the fury of the seas. For this work it was necessary not only to know the North Sea and the east coast of England but also the ports from the Netherlands to Norway. During these years he had also sailed through the English Channel and into the Irish Sea.

By 1755, although only twenty-seven years of age, Cook

had been promoted to Chief Mate of his ship, and only eleven years after having gone to sea, he was offered, by John Walker, the captaincy of a ship. It must have been a surprise to him and to Cook's other friends that he turned down this opportunity and volunteered for the Royal Navy as an ordinary seaman. As it turned out, many people around the world could be grateful that he acted as he did.

James Cook had, by this time, grown into a big man and was over 1.82 metres (six feet) tall, of striking appearance and a man of few words. He had become an outstanding seaman with great powers of observation and the ability for attention to endless detail. Geography fascinated him. He had a fearless interest in the world, in people and in wildlife in whatever area he was able to explore.

ROYAL NAVY

Life in the Royal Navy in 1755 was very hard. The average man-of-war carried 560 men in a space about the size of a small ferry boat. The seamen lived and slept on wet and windy gun-decks. Thirty-five centimetres (fourteen inches) abreast was the space allotted to sling a hammock. The death rate was very high, so, to keep the ships fully manned, there had to be men on board to replace those who would die at sea. Things were so terrible that the only way to get enough men on board was to use force. Men were drugged in hotels, made drunk or hit over the head and then they would wake up to find themselves out on the briny ''with a heaving stomach, a rolling deck and the sickening realization that they had been shanghaied''.

The life he had experienced on previous ships had been tough but in the Navy it was described as 'just survival'. On the first naval ship that Cook sailed in, 22 died at sea and 130 were put ashore in the first few months seriously ill with scurvy. In those days there was no refrigeration and so no way of keeping fruit and vegetables for long and it was the lack of fresh fruit and vegetables that caused this much dreaded disease that so frequently occurred amongst the men at sea.

The food was inferior salted meat; poor quality mouldy cheese; biscuits, peas and oatmeal which all had weevils in them and there was nothing else except a liberal grog issue of beer, rum and brandy to dull the senses of the seamen into the acceptance of their appalling conditions. Is it any wonder that surprise was registered when this 27-year-old man volunteered for service in the Royal Navy.

A month after he joined the navy as ordinary seaman, he was promoted to the rank of Boatswain (Bo'sun). For this position a man had to know his ship and the sea, because he was responsible for the care of the masts, yards, sails, rigging, anchors, boats and cordage. A man in this position had a high-pitched whistle that was often used to give orders to the crew, as it could be heard above the roar of the storms. This whistle is still used on board ship on ceremonial occasions.

There was much that Cook did not like about the naval practices and conditions of those days but, whatever his own feelings, he was ready to obey those in command. This is a necessary ability in anybody who is to become a leader. Later, he was to have the opportunity to apply his own ideas about discipline and the treatment of his men.

FIRST COMMAND

It was not long before he received his first command. It

was a small, twelve-metre (forty-foot) sloop which was part of a convoy. It was on this sloop that he proved to his seniors — and more important, to himself — that, under extreme strain, he could still cope with all the difficult situations with which he was faced and cope in such a way that he won respect from his men.

When he joined the Navy, the Seven Years' War had just started and he was involved in it from the beginning to the end. For the first two years, he was engaged in the endless patrolling of the east coast of England. There he practised intense watchfulness in raging storms as well as in fair weather.

At that time many men who had little ability for the work reached high positions through recommendation from influential friends or through money. Cook had proved himself worthy of higher positions and had been recommended by men who were knowledgeable about ships and yet he chose to do the qualifying examinations and won his Master's Certificate in his own right. This meant that he was qualified to command His Majesty's ships.

MASTER

His first command as Master gave him the task of patrolling further north — the east coast of Scotland and the Orkney and Shetland Islands. After several months he was transferred to another ship and, as a result, in 1757, he sailed for Canada. Not long after arriving there he had an experience that proved most helpful.

STRANGE MEETING

One day he went ashore and noticed a man carrying a table that was supported on a tripod. He watched him and saw that he set it up, looked along the top of the table and then made notes. He soon got into conversation with this man, who was a Major Samuel Holland, and learnt that he was surveying the area. As it turned out, Holland instructed Cook in the science of surveying and this was to lead to Cook's outstanding work in this field. In the course of time, it was found out that Holland was born in the same year as Cook; that at the age of seventeen, when Cook became apprenticed to John Walker, Holland, who was Dutch, joined the Dutch army; that in 1755, when Cook joined the navy, Holland had come to England and had been commissioned in the British army; that they had both been sent to Canada at the same time and that, though one was in the navy and the other in the army, they met on the banks of the St. Lawrence between two battles.

In 1759 Cook played an important roll in the expedition led by General Wolfe that gained Canada as a British colony. Under the cover of night he had marked out a safe channel up the dangerous St. Lawrence River by placing buoys at the danger points.

STUDY

Unlike his brother officers, Cook did not relax with a pint of flip (a mixture of spirits and beer). Every spare moment was taken up with study. His study on and off duty turned out to be necessary for his future. The same independence and ability to go his own way whatever other people were doing that had shown up when he was at school, showed up again now. He maintained this strength all his life and it is just as well for his men that he did. Many times he had to be ready to make decisions on which the life of the men depended and he had to be ready to make them at any time of the day or night — even immediately after being woken up.

RESPONSIBILITY

And so it was that this young man, for he was only in his early thirties, became the most skilled pilot in the navy, Master of the Admiral's ship and a very accomplished surveyor. When the war came to an end, Cook returned to England and was discharged from his ship but not from the Navy.

Lord Colville, the Captain of Cook's ship, while addressing the Admiralty said, "Mr. Cook late Master of the *Northumberland* acquainted me that he has laid before their Lordships all his drafts and observations relating to the River St. Lawrence, part of the coast of Nova Scotia and of Newfoundland.

"On this occasion, I beg leave to inform their Lordships that from my experience of Mr Cook's genius and capacity, I think him well qualified for the work performed, and for greater undertakings of the same kind — these drafts being made under my own eye I can venture to say, they may be the means of directing many in the right way, but cannot mislead any."

In 1762, after he was discharged from the *Northumberland*, when he was in his thirty-fifth year, he married Elizabeth Batts. She was a girl from Barking in Essex and she was twenty-one. Five months after they were married his duties again took him away from England.

CANADA

SURVEYING

From 1763 to 1768 every summer, the time when the country was not subjected to snow and ice, James Cook's work was to survey the new country that was now the possession of England. He became the Engineering-Surveyor of Newfoundland and his works are still preserved to this day. It was important to Britain that Newfoundland should be surveyed as it was there that the fishing trade was opened up and an accurate survey of the dangerous coast and harbours became a necessity. Combining his knowledge of charting the coasts from the sea with surveying on land Cook's maps were a work of art and they were accepted by the Royal Society. The Royal Society, since 1660, has been responsible for the preservation of scientific knowledge as it came to hand and it was and still is considered an honour by anyone to have his work accepted. About his work at this time it has been said, "Cook was to carry out many accomplished pieces of surveying, in one part of the world or another, but nothing he ever did later exceeded in accomplishment his surveys of the southern and western sides of Newfoundland from 1765 to 1767."

We are told that one hundred years later, during which time many men had charted that part of Canada, including the Gulf of St. Lawrence, professional hydrographers studying existing maps decided that many were so inaccurate that they were dangerous to seamen. They destroyed them all except those done by Cook and Lane, who was one of his assistants.

SCIENCE

As we know James Cook had always been interested in mathematics and he was able to apply it to his surveying, charting and navigating and he was also able to apply it to the study of astronomy. In 1766 he took an accurate sighting of an eclipse of the sun and this brought him recognition amongst astronomers.

By this time he already had more achievements to his name

than any other man of the sea. He had proved himself to be reliable not only in seafaring on the dangerous waters off England and Canada but also in surveying and astronomy, observation and calculation.

EXPLORATION

At the age of forty, James Cook was about to set out to sail across the oceans of the world. His name is so closely associated with the discovery of islands in the Pacific Ocean, particularly with his discovery of the largest island, that people tend to forget that he also rediscovered and charted the coasts of the North and South Islands of New Zealand, charted the west coast of North America, Canada and Alaska and part of the west coast of Siberia as well as the east coast of Australia. He also sailed into the ice-fields of the Arctic and Antarctic Circles and sailed farther south than anybody before.

ASTRONOMY

At this time, great interest was starting up in all sciences: including botany, astronomy, geography and zoology. There was also now a need for men at sea to be able to calculate their position more accurately.

It was known that on June 3rd 1769 there would be an important event occurring in the skies. This was the *Transit of Venus* across the face of the sun. The astronomers knew that if they could get accurate information about this from different places, they could get valuable help in calculating the distance of the earth from the sun and that this in turn would help to calculate longitude at sea.

From the Royal Society came the decision about which

places were to be used to get this information. The event was to be observed from three different locations. One was North Cape, on the tip of Scandinavia in the Arctic Circle; the second was Port Churchill, on Hudson Bay in Canada and the third was the newly discovered island of Tahiti in the Pacific Ocean. For this scientific purpose, there was a need for someone with astronomical experience to go to Tahiti.

DISCOVERY

Before Cook's time, it was practically impossible to determine the exact location of a newly discovered land or ship in the middle of a vast ocean. The latitude — that is the north-south location — could be determined but the longitude — the east-west location — presented great problems. Before it was possible to calculate longitude with any degree of exactitude and in a reasonable time, the necessary work had to be done by mathematicians, astronomers and by at least

A CHRONOMETER SIMILAR TO THAT INVENTED BY JOHN HARRISON WHICH CAPTAIN COOK TOOK WITH HIM ON HIS SECOND AND THIRD VOYAGES

one inventor, who had to invent a timepiece capable of keeping accurate time under all conditions. The successful inventor was John Harrison and his famous invention was the chronometer. The necessary work was more or less completed by 1768. With all new knowledge, there are few who can use it at first. Cook was able to use it, because in him a scientific turn of mind was combined with first-class seamanship and an intense interest in being of service in the work of locating new lands. The methods established by him were passed on to Bligh and others and from Bligh to Flinders.

For many hundreds of years seafaring men from different countries had ventured into the Pacific Ocean and had already sighted some land but, so far, the largest land mass remained undiscovered. Some thought it stretched all the way from New Guinea to South America and from the Solomon Islands right down to Antarctica. Torres had actually seen the northern tip of Australia when he saw what is now known as Cape York. The Dutch had charted some of the west coast but did not think it was worth following up, as they were only interested in trade. Tasman had seen what he thought to be the southern tip when he sighted land to the north of where he was sailing. Actually he had circumnavigated Australia without ever seeing it, except for the southern tip.

CHOICE OF LEADER

Just at the time when the Royal Society wanted someone to go to Tahiti, the Admiralty wanted someone to do further exploration in the Pacific. It was decided to combine the two ventures. Naturally there was a need for a man who had proved himself to be a good observer of the stars, a good sailor, a good navigator and a good commander. They could have chosen someone good at all these tasks who was an arrogant man with a very bad temper and little concern for the health of the men. Though there were other qualified men, James Cook was chosen. The choice of Cook was a wise one because it put the men in close touch with a leader for whom they could have the greatest respect.

PREPARATION

It must have been pleasing to Cook that his advice was accepted with regard to the choosing of the ship. A Whitby-built 'bark', — there is a difference between a 'bark' and a 'barque' — which had formerly been used as a collier, was chosen for the venture. It was purchased for the sum of $5,000 (£2,840) weighed 373 tonnes (368 tons), was 29.8 metres (98 feet) long and had a maximum beam of 8.9 metres (29 feet three inches). In fact it was only the size of a ferry boat and it carried a crew of 94.

THE HULL OF THE *ENDEAVOUR*, by Sydney Parkinson

A voyage such as the one planned placed tremendous strains on the captain, for he had the responsibility not only for the ship but also for each man on board. Cook took these responsibilities with the greatest seriousness and this makes all the difference. There can be no greater strain on a kind and serious man than the making of countless decisions affecting the lives of others. Giving orders does no harm to the health of an egotistic, bombastic peson but is a continuing strain on the health of one who, aware of constant danger, has to give orders that can be a matter of life or death to others and this was what lay ahead of him.

His concern for the men under his command led him to prepare in such a way as to try to prevent the diseases so common at sea. Up to this time, many men had died at sea because of a complete lack of fresh fruit and vegetables for long stretches of time as well as the general conditions on the ships. He planned what stores had to be loaded. These included fowls, pickled cabbage, oranges, lemons, malt, sassafras and wild celery. Added to all this there was a goat which had been given to Cook as a present by Captain Wallis, who had recently returned from discovering Tahiti. He gave him the goat he had taken to ensure a supply of fresh milk.

Cook planned to bring in three meatless meals a week, to see that rigorous attention was paid to the ventilation of the men's quarters, to the cleanliness of the ship and to the cooking utensils as well as ensuring the cleanliness of the men. Regular baths of cold sea water would be compulsory. He also planned to shorten the watches from two twelve-hour to three eight-hour watches, giving the seamen breaks such as they had never had before.

As if the strain and stress would not be enough, some

unimaginative organizer gave permission for a botanist, Joseph Banks, with a party of eight other men, to go along on the voyage. They could not be asked to take up their abode in the crew's quarters so, into the minute officers' quarters they had to be crowded.

What a shock it must have been to the Captain of this long voyage to see the cluttered assembly of scientists boarding his already overladen ship. These persons and their belongings were to share his Great Cabin, a thing just not done in the Navy. The Great Cabin was the 'commander's only and very necessary place of privacy, especially on a long voyage. This meant that the ship's only large room, serving as the captain's chart-room, messroom, library and writing room was practically unavailable to Cook.

FIRST VOYAGE

So, at 2 p.m. August 26th 1768, Captain James Cook sailed the *Endeavour*, as the bark was named, from Plymouth — in the wake of Magellan — towards the destroying seas of Cape Horn.

They were only seven days at sea when the *Endeavour* ran into a storm in the Bay of Biscay. Cook reports, 'washed overboard a small boat belonging to the boatswain and drowned between three and four dozen of our poultry which was worst of all.' The fowls were to provide eggs for the sick and then, after their laying days were over, they would provide fresh meat.

The first landfall was made at Madeira and there they spent a pleasant stay of six days whilst fruit and vegetables, including 13.6 kilos (30lbs) of onions per man and fresh water were taken aboard. Here Mr. Weir, the first mate, was dragged overboard by the anchor rope and drowned.

Then they set out across the Atlantic to South America to make port at Rio de Janiero, the last civilized port of call for over two years. The Military Governor could not believe that a Whitby collier with so few guns was a King's ship. He suspected that they were smugglers and so restricted landing to those who could be guarded. They were allowed to replenish stores and to have work done on the ship.

Unfortunately another good seaman, Peter Flower, who had been with Cook for five years, was drowned at Rio. (Few sailors could swim in those days and did not wish to learn, preferring the quick death by drowning to the prolonged ordeal of swimming for hours.) Some specimens were collected by Banks who, going against the Governor's orders, spent the day, undetected, by getting ashore before dawn and returning after dark. It must have been a relief to the Captain to clear the unwelcoming port.

CAPE HORN

The *Endeavour* was then headed south to follow the South American coastline to the dreaded Cape Horn. Whilst rounding it through the Straits of Le Maire, Banks chose to go ashore in seas recognized by Cook to be highly dangerous. This left them hanging on to an almost impossible anchorage waiting for his return the following morning. This little venture of Banks cost the lives of his two servants and left the rest of the shore party almost dead from exhaustion and exposure. Banks, with his lack of knowledge of handling a sailing ship in dangerous waters, was later to add considerably to the difficulties of Cook's expedition. Cook had no command over Banks and had to fit in with many of his requests, though, at times he was asking what was almost impossible.

TAHITI

The *Endeavour* rounded the Horn without further mishap and sailed a greater distance south-west than any ship had been before. Then Cook brought his ship about and, with only the rough charts of Captain Wallis to guide him, headed for the warmer seas of the South Pacific to search for Tahiti, the largest island in the group Cook was to call the Society Isles, but still just a tiny speck on the vast ocean.

At dawn on April 13th 1769, without the aid of modern nautical instruments, this remarkable navigator dropped anchor in Matavai Bay as smiling Tahitians welcomed them with gifts of fruit and coconuts and their calls of ''taio! taio! (friend).

Seven weeks later a successful observation of *The Transit of Venus* was undertaken. However, it was not till August 9th that, to the wailing laments of the Tahitians, the *Endeavour* shipped anchor, taking a little bit of Tahiti with her. This was Tupia, a former Raiatean high priest, and a skilled navigator of the Polynesian Islands. Tupia was signed on as pilot and interpreter. He was to be a big help as a guide through the numerous atolls and as an interpreter of the Polynesian language, which is spoken in all the Pacific Islands.

NEW ZEALAND

The *Endeavour* then sailed south in search of New Zealand and the tropical warmth was all too soon replaced by the cold trade winds, which caused the death of live stock that had been taken on board in Tahiti. For just on two months, Cook searched for what Tasman had seen 127 years before and on 6th October land was sighted. He landed at what is now known as Poverty Bay, in the North Island and claimed New Zealand for Britain.

He had difficulty in persuading the natives that they were friendly. In spite of the fact that Maoris they first contacted were found to be very intelligent though hostile and cannibalistic, Cook did achieve a friendly relationship and was able to maintain it. They spoke the Polynesian language, which added to the advantage of having Tupia on board. Cook became a legendary figure amongst the Maoris.

A Maori Chief, who was a boy when he saw Captain Cook, said, fifty years later, "There was one supreme man in the ship. We knew he was chief of the whole mission by his perfect gentlemanly and noble demeanour. He seldom spoke, but some of his 'goblins' spoke much. He came to us and patted our cheeks and gently touched our heads. My companions said, 'This is the leader, which is proved by his kindness to us...A noble man cannot be lost in a crowd.' "

THE ANTIPODES

During the next six months, Cook circumnavigated the two islands. Villiers makes it perfectly clear what sort of problems confronted Cook.

"So he began that extraordinary circumnavigation of both islands of New Zealand which, even in his spectacular seafaring career, was an outstanding achievement. He had to sail over 2,500 miles (4,000 kilometres) in difficult water off a

CHARTING THE NEW ZEALAND COAST

dangerous and unknown coast, much of it exposed to the Roaring Forties, extending to within a few degrees of the latitude of Cape Horn. He had to make as good a survey as he could. He had to do all this with a single ship and no means of communication. He was at the Antipodes, as far from base as a European ship could get: if he were lost no one would know where to look for him. His ship was a small square-rigged ship, lightly sparred, which had already been sailing for over a year; yet there he was, pitting her and her people against the Roaring Forties and the Tasman Sea — two notorious breeders of bad weather — and determined to stay upon that coast until he had put it on the world map no matter how long it took or what the difficulties.

''A sailing-ship Master compelled to coast with the wind blowing onshore, had to keep off or risk wreck; yet if Cook did not sail close in, no one would learn much. Submerged rocks licking their ship-tearing edges just below the surface were difficult to see: ledges of them could be anywhere. To sail into what looked like harbours, even after the Master had done some sounding from a boat, meant some element of risk, and doing things which the prudent seaman most dislikes having to do. Cook was above all else a prudent seaman. He had to be audacious too: if he did not investigate harbours he would never find a base or haven to gather wild celery and other essential anti-scorbutics, or for rest for the people (Maoris permitting) and the chance to cut wood and collect water. These he had to have: the demand was almost insatiable. If the wind was offshore he could be blown away, and often was: then he must fight his way back again. If there was no wind at all the ship had to stay where she was, at anchor if possible, or drift at the mercy of current or tide. She could anchor only where the depth of sea permitted her anchors to reach the bottom, and the bottom must offer good holding...

"The plain everyday difficulties of handling these ships, though the last engineless Cape Horners went out of commission only in 1950, are already so forgotten as to seem incredible. Their means of movement was the wind properly directed to their sails: yet they did not accept the mercy or the vagaries of the wind. They had to *fight* for their way, fight for their lives at times. To them lee shores were anathema and onshore winds on rocky coasts the threat of death. Cook had good boats, of course: but even with twenty stout men in each of the two best they could tow only in still water or with a favouring current. A small ship could make some progress slowly in flat water — up rivers, or in winding harbours — by what sailors called 'kedging', which meant carrying a light anchor ahead by boat and throwing it overboard, then hauling the ship up to it, then carrying another anchor further again, hauling to that, and so on. This was of no use in the open sea.

"No, a sailing-ship Master compelled to work his ship even on a familiar coast must often have his heart in his mouth. When Cook came there the New Zealand coast was familiar to no man. Tasman had not even landed except once briefly on an offshore island. The *Endeavour* touched perilously on a submerged rock, brushed a cliff with her lee yardarms (fortunately the cliff was steep-to) while beating away from sudden peril caused by a shift of flukey wind, blew out some of her best sails, narrowly avoided wreck by night on a reef of offshore rocks near Stewart Island (Cook named them The Traps, with good reason) and again by day in that windy place Cook Straits, where only a desperate anchoring saved her when a strong tide pushed her broadside towards more rocks in a calm. Cook Straits had a bad name throughout the sailing-ship era."

While charting this dangerous but beautiful coast, Cook had his most serious split with Banks. Banks and Solander, a naturalist, asked Cook to enter a precipitous fjord to make a landing. This time, Cook refused. The fjord was too deep for an anchorage and a stiff inshore breeze was blowing. Cook saw the risk of foundering his ship and sacrificing his men and the expedition at this farthermost point from Britain. Banks readily wrote of the incident in his journal in which he also wrote remarks belittling his Captain. It says a lot for Cook that at the end of the voyage he and Banks were on friendly terms.

Having completed the charting of the two islands, they left New Zealand from Cape Farewell on 31st March 1770. Cook now studied all the different accounts of the men who had, over the years, sailed into the southern waters and then decided to set his course west. For two weeks, he sailed west.

AUSTRALIA

On the 16th April, they met bad weather coming from the south. It was the bad weather that caused Cook to travel farther north than he had intended. He had been heading for what is now known as Bass Strait but, because they went farther north, land was sighted On 18th April at 6.00 a.m., Lieutenant Hicks sighted land to the north, land which ran east west. To this southernmost tip of Australia, Cook gave the name Point Hicks but it has since been changed to Cape Everard.

What he had discovered turned out to be the long-searched-for *Terra Australis* which was to be called Australia.

CHARTING THE COAST

Cook now started the task of charting this coastline. It was very dangerous work. At first he had no idea of how dangerous it was. The actual coastline of Australia is some 21,000 kilometres (13,000) miles and Cook was to chart the first 3,200 kilometres (2,000 miles) before turning for home. As they sailed up the coast, some distance from the shore, he named many of the prominent features. At night, he would go farther out to sea, because of the strong surf beating against the shore. The next day, he would go inshore again. As they passed what is now known as Jervis Bay, the weather was not good, so they went farther north. They made their first attempt at landing at a place which is thought to have been where Bulli now is.

LANDING IN AUSTRALIA

The next morning at daybreak, a bay was sighted and in the afternoon Cook took the ship into it. It was 29th April 1770.

Botany Bay is the name given by Cook himself to this historic place. The actual landing site is now called Kurnell.

As the party that was to make the landing approached the shore, Cook turned to Isaac Smith, who had joined his crew as a fifteen-year-old boy, and said, "Isaac, you shall land first." This boy was to become a rear-admiral in the British Navy.

The landing party held a short ceremony and they were watched by some Aborigines. This was a ceremony that was to be mimed by them many times in their corroborees. How strange it must have seemed to them. How strange to see such apparitions from the huge monster with the white wings!

THE LANDING PLACE AT KURNELL, BOTANY BAY

These ancient people were entirely different from the many natives with whom Cook had had contact. They were not interested in the trading trinkets shown to them. They, the most primitive people left on earth, wanted nothing more than they already had and to be left alone with their 'dreaming time' and ancient Aboriginal mythology. Their speech was absolutely different from the Polynesian and was as strange to Tupia as it was to the Europeans. Contact could only be made by making signs.

Banks and the naturalists were enchanted by the bay, with

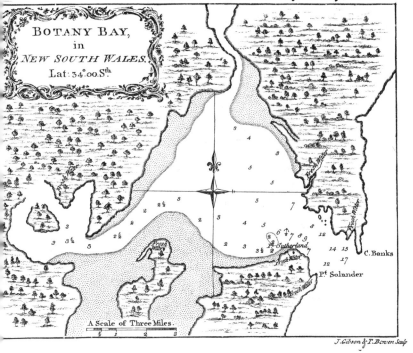

CHART OF BOTANY BAY, 1770, engraved by J. Gibson and T. Bowen

37

the stately gum trees, beautiful birds and unusual animals and soon every available portion of the ship, including what little was left of the Great Cabin, was full of botanical specimens.

Forby Sutherland, a seaman from the Orkney Islands died of consumption and became the first white man to be buried in Australia, in what is now Sutherland Shire.

FURTHER CHARTING

Eight days after landing in this far off country, Cook continued up the coast, charting as he went. Experiencing good weather they passed by what is now Sydney Harbour and Cook made the note that there was a "Bay or Harbour, wherein there appeared to be a safe anchorage". It was he who named it Port Jackson. He then noted the bay on which Newcastle now stands and so on up the coast, observing and naming. Then they came to a very dangerous section which he named Point Danger. On looking inland he saw a high peak which he called Mount Warning. Those who have visited Byron Bay, which is the part of Australia first touched by the rays of the rising sun, will have seen the Captain Cook Lighthouse. They will also have seen Mount Warning 1,556 metres (5,105 feet) high. Of the reef that runs out from Point Danger Cook said, "These reefs may always be known by the peaked mountain which bears from them south-west. For this reason I have named it Mount Warning."

Sailing north more bays were named and many days of calm sailing experienced. Then there appeared on the horizon numerous islands and the depth of the sea kept changing dramatically. For about the next 1,600 kilometres (1,000 miles) Cook had to pick his way, by countless soundings, over the jagged coral reef, during which time he went on charting the east coast of Australia and named more prominent features. He was certainly using his experience gained in the 'nursery of seamen' and he must have been pleased to have the Whitby collier with its broad bottom and stout timbers. They had entered what we now know as The Great Barrier Reef. At first the reef was well out to sea but there were many islands to be steered past. However, as they sailed farther north, it closed in towards the coast. They sailed through Whitsunday Passage and on up past Green Island, which he named. Then, on the 10th June at 11.00 p.m., while sailing under perfect conditions on a moonlight night in deep water, disaster struck. The story of the incident is given in Cook's own words.

FROM COOK'S JOURNAL

We had the advantage of a fine breeze, and a clear moonlight night, and in standing off from six till near nine o'clock, we deepened our water from fourteen to twenty-one fathom, but while we were at supper it suddenly shoaled, and we fell into twelve, ten, and eight fathom, within the space of a few minutes; I immediately ordered every body to their station, and all was ready to put about and come to an anchor, but meeting at the next cast of the lead with deep water again, we concluded that we had gone over the tail of the shoals which we had seen at sun-set, and that all danger was past: before ten, we had twenty and one and twenty fathom, and before the lead could be cast again, the ship struck, and remained immoveable, except by the heaving of the surge, that beat her against the craggs of the rock upon which she lay.

In a few moments every body was upon the deck, with countenances which sufficiently expressed the horrors of our situation. We had stood off the shore three hours and a half, with a pleasant breeze, and therefore knew that we could not be very near it, and we had too much reason to conclude that we were upon a rock of coral, which is more fatal than any other, because the points of it are sharp, and every part of the surface so rough as to grind away whatever is rubbed against it, even with the gentlest motion. In this situation all the sails were immediately taken in, and the boats hoisted out to examine the depth of water round the ship: we soon discovered that our fears had not aggravated our misfortune, and that the vessel had been lifted over a ledge of the rock, and lay in a hollow within it: in some places there was from three to four fathom, and in others not so many feet.

THE *ENDEAVOUR* ON THE CORAL REEF

As soon as the long-boat was out, we struck our yards and top-masts, and carried out the stream anchor on the starboard bow, got the coasting anchor and cable into the boat...having taken ground, our utmost force was applied to the capstan, hoping that if the anchor did not come home, the ship would be got off, but to our great misfortune and disappointment we could not move her: during all this time she continued to beat with great violence against the rock, so that it was with the utmost difficulty that we *kept upon our legs; and to complete the scene of distress, we saw by the light of the moon the sheathing boards from the bottom of the vessel floating away all round her, and at last her false keel, so that every moment was making way for the sea to rush in which was to swallow us up.*

We had now no chance but to lighten her, and we had lost the opportunity of doing that to the greatest advantage, for unhappily we went on shore just at high water, and by this time it had considerably fallen, so that after she should be lightened so as to draw as much less water as the water had sunk, we should be but in the same situation as at first; and the only alleviation of this circumstance was, that as the tide ebbed the ship settled to the rocks, and was not beaten against them with so much violence.

This however was no time to indulge conjecture, nor was any effort remitted in despair of success: that no time might be lost, the water was immediately started in the hold, and pumped up; six of our guns, being all we had upon the deck, our iron and stone ballast, casks, hoop staves, oil jars, decayed stores, and many other things that lay in the way of heavier materials, were thrown overboard with the utmost expedition, every one exerting himself with an alacrity almost approaching to cheerfulness, with the least repining or discontent; yet the men were so far imprest with a sense of their situation, that not an oath was heard among them, the habit of profaneness, however strong, being instantly subdued, by the dread of incurring guilt when death seemed to be so near.

While we were thus employed, day broke upon us, and we saw the land at about eight leagues distance, without any island in the intermediate space, upon which, if the ship should have gone to pieces, we might have been set ashore by the boats, and from which they might have taken us by different turns to the main: the wind however gradually died away, and early in the forenoon it was a dead calm; if it had blown hard, the ship must inevitably have been

41

destroyed. At eleven in the forenoon we expected high water, and anchors were got out, and every thing made ready for another effort to heave her off if she should float, but to our inexpressible surprize and concern she did not float by a foot and a half, though we had lightened her near fifty ton, so much did the day-tide fall short of that in the night.

We now proceeded to lighten her still more, and threw over-board every thing that it was possible for us to spare: hitherto she had not admitted much water, but as the tide fell, it rushed in so fast, that two pumps, incessantly worked, could scarely keep her free. At two o'clock, she lay heeling two or three streaks to starboard, and the pinnace, which lay under her bows, touched the ground: we had now no hope but from the tide at midnight...

About five o'clock in the afternoon, we observed the tide begin to rise, but we observed at the same time that the leak had gained upon us so considerably, that it was imagined she must go to the bottom as soon as she ceased to be supported by the rock: this was a dreadful circumstance, so that we anticipated the floating of the ship not as an earnest of deliverance, but as an event that would probably precipitate our destruction.

We well knew that our boats were not capable of carrying us all on shore, and that when the dreadful crisis should arrive, as all command and subordination would be at an end, a contest for preference would probably ensue, that would increase the horrors even of shipwreck, and terminate in the destruction of us all by the hands of each other; yet we knew that if any should be left on board to perish in the waves, they would probably suffer less upon the whole that those who should get on shore....

To those only who have waited in a state of such suspense, death has approached in all his terrors; and as the dreadful moment that was to determine our fate came on, every one saw his own sensations pictured in the countenances of his companions; however, the capstan and windlace were manned with as many hands as could be spared from the pumps, and the ship floating about twenty minutes after ten o'clock, the effort was made, and she was heaved into deep water.

It was some comfort to find that she did not now admit more water than she had done upon the rock; and though, by the gaining of the leak upon the pumps, there was no less than three feet nine inches (109 centimetres) water in the hold, yet the men did not relinquish their labour, and we held the water as it were at bay; but having now endured excessive fatigue of body and agitation of mind for more than four and twenty hours, and having but little hope of succeeding at last, they began to flag: none of them could work at the pump more that five or six minutes together, and then, being totally exhausted, they threw themselves down upon the deck, though a stream of water was running over it from the pumps between three and four inches (eight and ten centimetres) deep; when those who succeeded them had worked their spell, and were exhausted in their turn, they threw themselves down in the same manner, and the others started up again, and renewed their labour; thus relieving each other till an accident was very near putting an end to their efforts at once.

The planking which lines the inside of the ship's bottom is called the ceiling, and between this, and the outside planking, there is a space of about eighteen inches (45 centimetres): the man who till this time had attended the well to take the depth of water, had taken it only to the ceiling, and gave the measure accordingly; but he being now relieved, the person who came in his stead, reckoned the depth to the outside planking, by which it appeared in a few minutes to have gained upon the pumps eighteen inches (45centimetres), the difference between the planking without and within. Upon this, even the bravest was upon the point of giving up his labour with his *hope, and in a few minutes every thing would have been involved in all the confusion of despair.*

But this accident, however dreadful in its first consequences, was eventually the cause of our preservation: the mistake was soon detected, and the sudden joy which every man felt upon finding his situation better than his fears had suggested, operated like a charm, and seemed to possess him with a strong belief that scarcely any real danger remained. New confidence and new hope, however founded, inspired new vigour; and though our state was the same as when the men first began to slacken in their labour, through weariness and despondency, they now renewed their efforts with such alacrity and spirit, that before eight o' clock in the morning the leak was so far from having gained upon the pumps, that the pumps had gained considerably upon the leak.

It was however impossible long to continue the labour by which the pumps had been made to gain upon the leak, and as the exact situation of it could not be discovered, we had no hope of stopping it within. In this situation, Mr. Monkhouse, one of my midshipmen, came to me and proposed an expedient that he had once seen used on board a merchant ship, which sprung a leak that admitted four feet (1.2 metres) an hour, and which by this expedient was brought safely from Virginia to London; the master having such confidence in it, that he took her out of harbour, knowing her condition, and did not think it worth while to wait till the leak could be otherwise stopped.

To this man, therefore, the care of the expedient, which is called fothering the ship, was immediately committed, four or five of the people being appointed to assist him, and he performed it in this manner: He took a lower studding sail, and having mixed together a large quantity of oakham and wool, chopped pretty small, he stitched it down in handfuls upon the sail, as lightly as possible, *and over this he spread the dung of our sheep and other filth; but horse dung, if we had had it, would have been better. When the sail was thus prepared, it was hauled under the ship's bottom by ropes, which kept it extended, and when it came under the leak, the suction which carried in the water, carried in with it the oakham and wool from the surface of the sail, which in other parts the water was not sufficiently agitated to wash off.*

By the success of this expedient our leak was so far reduced, that instead of gaining upon three pumps, it was easily kept under with one. This was a new source of confidence and comfort;...

Upon this occasion I must observe, both in justice and gratitude to the ship's company, and the Gentlemen on board, that although in the midst of our distress every one seemed to have a just sense of his danger, yet no passionate exclamations, or frantic gestures, were to be heard or seen; every one appeared to have the perfect possession of his mind, and every one exerted himself to the uttermost, with a quiet and patient perseverance, equally distant from the tumultuous violence of terror, and the gloomy inactivity of despair.

They gingerly edged in towards the mainland and it took two days to reach a favourable anchorage well off shore. The small boats were sent out to try and find a safe harbour.

The pinnace was still out with one of the mates; but at nine o'clock she returned, and reported, that about two leagues (eleven kilometres) *to leeward she had discovered just such a harbour as we wanted, in which there was a sufficient rise of water, and every other convenience that could be desired, either for laying the ship ashore, or heaving her down.*

I went myself and buoyed the channel, which I found very narrow; the harbour also I found smaller than I expected, but most excellently adapted to our purpose; and it is remarkable, that in the whole course of our voyage we had seen no place which, in our present circumstances, could have afforded us the same relief.

However, a further three days passed before the weather allowed them to enter the bay through the narrow channel. On the way through the ship went aground twice. Not once were they out of danger of the coral reef until the ship was in the harbour, which was actually the mouth of a river. By then it was 16th June and they stayed there till 4th August. This river he named Endeavour River and Cooktown, Queensland, now stands on it.

THE ENTRANCE TO THE ENDEAVOUR RIVER

There was much to do in setting up camp, looking after the sick, getting food and establishing as good as possible a relationship with the native people. Five days passed before Cook was able to examine the ship.

At two o'clock in the morning of the 22nd, the tide left her, and gave us an opportunity to examine the leak, which we found to be at her floor heads, a little before the starboard fore-chains. In this place the rocks had made their way through four planks, and even into the timbers; three more planks were much damaged, and the appearance of these breaches was very extraordinary: there was not a splinter to be seen, but all was as smooth, as if the whole had been cut away by an instrument: the timbers in this place were happily very close, and if they had not, it would have been absolutely impossible to have saved the ship.

But after all, her preservation depended upon a circumstance still more remarkable: in one of the holes, which was big enough to have sunk us, if we had had eight pumps instead of four, and been able to keep them incessantly going, was in great measure plugged up by a fragment of the rock, which, after having made the wound, was left sticking in it; so that the water which at first had gained upon our pumps, was what came in at the interstices, between the stone and the edges of the hole that received it. We found also several pieces of the fothering, which had made their way between the timbers, and in a great measure stopped those parts of the leak which the stone had left open.

Upon further examination, we found that, besides the leak, considerable damage had been done to the bottom; great part of the sheathing was gone from under the larboard bow; a considerable part of the false keel was also wanting, and these indeed we had seen swim away in fragments from the vessel, while she lay beating against the rock: the remainder of it was in so shattered a condition that it had better have been gone, and the fore foot and main keel were also damaged, but not so as to produce any immediate danger: what damage she might have received abaft could not yet be exactly known, but we had reason to think it was not much, as but little water made its way into her bottom, while the tide kept below the leak which has already been described.

By nine o'clock in the morning the carpenters got to work upon her, while the smiths were busy in making bolts and nails. In the mean time, some of the people were sent on the other side of the water to shoot pigeons for the sick, who at their return reported that they had seen an animal as large as a greyhound, of a slender make, a mouse colour, and extremely swift; they discovered also many Indian houses, and a fine stream of fresh water...

ENDEAVOUR RIVER

The crew had many weeks in tropical Australia repairing the ship. Food was plentiful, native spinach, beans growing along the river, kangaroos and birds were in abundance and the bay supplied turtles, clams and fish. However, the food reserve for the ship could not be built up as the Aboriginals provided constant opposition. They started bushfires around them and did everything they could to hasten the unwelcome visitors on their way.

LEAVING AUSTRALIA

Before leaving, Cook had men climb every vantage point to try to see if there was a way through the shoals, islands and coral reefs. He also sent men out in the small boats to see if they could find a way out. The ship left with sufficient rations to reach the Indies, as Indonesia was then called, but any further misadventure could have meant disaster. In spite of being constantly on the lookout there were many narrow escapes. It was not until 21st August that they passed the northern tip of the east coast which he named Cape York.

They had to creep every inch of the way until they had passed the Gulf of Carpentaria and had cleared the most northern point of Australia. After months of torturous movement over jagged spears of coral, everything seemed fair sailing.

They briefly touched the coast of New Guinea but spent little time there. We get a further insight into Cook's attitude to the native people he met in his travels from the following entry in his journal.

Soon after our return to the ship, we hoisted in the boat and made sail to the westward, being resolved to spend no more time upon this coast, to the great satisfaction of a very considerable majority of the ship's company. But I am sorry to say that I was strongly urged by some of the officers to send a party of men ashore, and cut down the cocoa-nut trees for the sake of the fruit. This I peremptorily refused, as equally unjust and cruel.

The natives had attacked us merely for landing upon their coast, when we attempted to take nothing away, and it was therefore morally certain that they would have made a vigorous effort to defend their property if it had been invaded, in which case many of them must have fallen a sacrifice to our attempt, and perhaps also some of our own people. I should have regretted the necessity of such a measure, if I had been in want of the necessaries of life; and certainly it would have been highly criminal when nothing was to be obtained but two or three hundred of green cocoa-nuts, which would at most have procured us a mere transient gratification.

JAVA

Java, civilization, and shore leave! To hear after two years of isolation what was happening in the world. It was here that Cook sent home his first dispatches telling of his discoveries and reporting a clean bill of health for his ship. Not to have any loss of life from scurvy after all that time at sea proved that it was helpful to the men that Cook insisted on them eating what he wanted them to eat. We are told that at first he resorted to the usual method of dealing with disobedience but after doing that once he resorted to other tactics and they worked. Cook gave the food he wanted the men to eat to the officers only. In a very short time the men were asking the Captain if it would not be possible for them to have some of that food too. It was in Java, a civilized port, that something came on board that Cook could not fight — civilization diseases.

HOMEWARD BOUND

As soon as possible Cook got his ship away from this port into clean waters again but the damage had been done and one man after another died. They died on the homeward track after they had successfully got through all that this exacting expedition could inflict upon them.

It is hard to imagine the feelings of the men as they committed their companions to the sea. To the Captain who had strained every nerve to guard the health of the men as well as to carry out his mission, each death must have brought both shock and sorrow. The first to die was the corporal of the marines, a man highly thought of by everyone on board. Then followed one of the naturalists, the artist, the sailmaker, then two from the carpenter's crew, the cook, the surgeon, Tupia, the carpenter himself and on it went. Only fifty-six men and the weather-beaten goat survived. At one time, on this gallant little ship only twelve men were active. The sorrow-stricken ship reached England on July 13th 1771.

RECEPTION

The *Endeavour* had been reported missing, presumed lost. Now this battered Whitby bark was sailing up the River Thames with all pennants flying. For this history-making expedition, Cook was mentioned in a small article in the *London Evening Post,* as having returned from a trip to the East Indies. This was the only recognition the press gave in spite of the high esteem in which he was held by the Admiralty and by the King. A week later, in the same newspaper, it was reported that Mr. Banks had discovered a Southern Continent. Other journals followed up with glowing reports of Mr. Banks and Mr. Solander's achievements in the cause of science and discovery. Cook was officially only a lieutenant and he remained so, whereas Mr. Banks subsequently received a knighthood.

HOMECOMING

Cook was not interested in the social life or the affairs of the Court. He returned to his home at Mile End Road, London, and it was only then that he learnt that his daughter, Elizabeth, had died three months earlier and that a son, Joseph, whom he had never seen, had died in infancy.

A SECOND VOYAGE

Cook did not have long at home. Preparations were soon being made for his second voyage, which was to take him right around the world. One of the purposes of this new voyage was to determine if *Terra Australis* did reach the South Pole. The venture was to use New Zealand as a base for the Polar part of the exploration.

It was decided that, since the *Endeavour* had proved to be of such sterling quality, the ships for the voyage would be built at Whitby and they were named *Resolution* and *Adventure*. The flagship, *Resolution*, was to be commanded by James Cook and the *Adventure* by Lieutenant Tobias Furneaux.

SOME HITCHES

It was intended that the whole expedition be commanded by Sir Joseph Banks. He had inherited a large income and had considerable political influence. He put in a request for an ornate three-decker passenger ship. It was refused by the Admiralty. However, a compromise was reached, allowing him to have a large, luxurious cabin put up above the deck on the *Resolution*. The shipbuilder protested and spoke about the effect of an upper deck on the stability of the ship and about the interference with the working of the sails. In spite of these protests from those who knew what they were talking about the deck was raised and the work completed. Banks' lack of knowledge about ships now became public. The ship almost rolled over with the weight of the additional top deck and had to be quickly restored to the original lines, at considerable expense not to mention the unfortunate delay.

After more demands from Banks, the Admiralty informed him that all further responsibility for the expedition was solely in the hands of Cook. Banks withdrew from the voyage but a man he chose was allowed to go as a scientist. This was John Forster of whom it is said that he was humourless, suspicious, demanding, rheumatic — a problem from any angle. This man was to receive a grant of $8,000 (£4,000). Cook was paid 60¢ (six shillings) a day. It was fortunate for everybody that this sort of thing did not worry Cook, who did not go in for criticism that would not help the work.

VOLUNTEERS

While it was a tragedy that Cook did not become known to large numbers of people it was clear that those who did know him were strongly attracted to him. Many of those with the spirit of adventure still burning in them joined the *Resolution* — if humanly possible. There were many young men on the *Resolution* who would become famous in their own right. George Vancouver, after whom the great city in Canada is named, was there as a fourteen-year-old midshipman; James Burney, who became a Fellow of the Royal Society, an excellent writer and a rear-admiral; Richard Grindall became a captain, fought under Nelson at the battle of Trafalgar and was then knighted and eventually became a vice-admiral; Joseph Gilbert, became a top surveyor, an excellent seaman and had the Gilbert Islands named after him. The Master of the *Resolution* was already an excellent seaman although he was only twenty-one. He was to take part in a famous mutiny, become a vice-admiral and the Governor of N.S.W. His name was William Bligh. It is obvious that the brave young men of the Royal Navy knew that in Cook they had an outstanding leader.

SETTING SAIL

The *Resolution* and the *Adventure* set sail from Plymouth Sound on July 13th 1772. They sailed south, passed Spain and the west coast of Africa and many observations were made. The men learned the routine of the ship, specially as regards what they were to eat as Cook again took the same precautions against scurvy. The ships called into Table Bay at the foot of Africa and on 22nd November, he set the course for the south and the Antarctic regions.

PIONEER SAILING

As Cook was to pioneer sailing in the ice-fields he had to learn much as he went along. They sailed through gales, squalls, fog, rain, snow and sleet and were lashed by heavy seas. While they thought of the icebergs as having an indescribable beauty they also realized that the danger was very great — only about one seventh of an iceberg is visible above the water. They were to sail into the Antarctic Circle before the weather forced them to turn north again.

They then continued their search for the unknown continent sailing east below where we now know this continent lies. Cook had the two ships sailing about 6.4 kilometres (four miles) apart so that the area of vision would be greater but nothing was seen until at last they sighted New Zealand again. By this time winter was upon them so, instead of waiting in New Zealand, Cook decided to sail in a circle around the Southern Pacific and in doing so he added more islands to the map.

Then he ventured into the Antarctic regions once more, going further south than any man before him. The perils of such voyages are well understood and are vividly described by Alan Villiers. In his book *The Seamen's Seaman* he gives the following description:-

THE *RESOLUTION* — IN ANTARCTICA , by William Hodges

ROUGH WEATHER

"Clear of the land, soon the wild westerly gales found them again, howling in the rigging and bringing up a vicious wintry sea in which the ships 'labour'd much', and the force of the rollers smashing at the rudder, jerked the tiller of the *Resolution* violently, flinging the helmsman right over the wheel — a nasty, bone-crushing habit sailing-ships running their easting down were to maintain until the end of the era. By good fortune, the helmsman so rudely thrown 'resembled a seal in substance and make' and so thwacked the deck like a 'bag of blubber'. The officer of the watch had immediately jumped to the wheel and held the spokes (or the rudder, banging wildly, might have smashed itself, or at least broken the tiller to pieces): the 'bag of blubber' picked himself up, no bones broken, and going back to the weather side, carried on grimly steering. Sudden mulish kicks from a square-rigger's wheel were always a risk, especially when running before a heavy sea. To guard against them, relieving tackles were rigged to restrain the tiller's tendency to jerk when a sea slapped the rudder, and the weather helmsman — he at the windward side of the wheel — wore a safety harness rigged stoutly to the deck, to hold him down. Men were sometimes thrown right overboard, or broke their limbs when hurled over the spinning spokes and smashed down on the wheel grating or the deck."

This was not all. Sometimes the weather itself, as the men headed farther south into previously unknown waters, was incredible and heroic efforts were needed to perform the essential tasks.

ANTARCTICA

"To touch the frozen rigging on frigid days was to risk

frost-burn which sears like flame: to fight those iron-hard sails aloft meant bloody hands and minced fingers, nails torn out by the roots and the hot blood swiftly frozen. This work could not be done with gloves. These men had no gloves — mittens at the wheel, yes: no gloves aloft. Canvas won't yield to gloves, and a sailing-ship sailor must have his 'feel' to do his work. In the intense cold with the frigid breath of frozen hell back-swept from the huge icebergs all round them, the human mechanism found places to freeze not hitherto thought of — the moisture in the eyes and in the nostrils, even among the hairs of the moustache and beard. Prosecute discoveries as near the South Pole as possible? What desk-bound bureau-crat wrote that? Discoveries of what? That cold hell long continued may be worse than burning?

"A good place for some bureaucrats, perhaps: but the bureaucrats were not there."

Time after time, grave danger threatened to destroy all of them. Time after time, only hard work and cool heads saved them but the strain was tremendous as they crossed beyond the edges of previously uncharted oceans. On another occas-ion while they were in warmer waters, a similar kind of self-discipline had been achieved in the presence of near disaster. This occasion resembled the crisis on the *Endeavour* on the first voyage. They were almost lost on a coral reef, and only their frantic efforts again saved the day. Sparrman, a botanist on board *Resolution*, recorded his impressions. "But even in my anxiety, I drew no small satisfaction from observing the rapidity and lack of confusion with which each command was executed to save the ship. No one seemed aware that he had been working for hours under a burning sun, the thermometer was 90° (32.2°Celsius) in the shade... As soon as the ship was once more afloat, I went down to the

Great Cabin with Captain Cook who, although he had from beginning to end of the incident appeared perfectly alert and able, was suffering so greatly from his stomach that he was in a great sweat and could scarcely stand.''

Cook then decided to sail north to Tahiti. After a short stay there he went on to name the New Hebrides, discover New Caledonia, sight what is now Norfolk Island and sail back to the base in New Zealand.

CIRCUMNAVIGATION

From there he headed home sailing east across the South Pacific Ocean. Instead of sailing below Cape Horn he sailed through the Magellan Strait for the first time from the west. This narrow winding stretch of water some 595 kilometres (370 miles) long, separates the mainland of South America from Tierra del Fuego and they spent a dangerous thirty-six days of constant watchfulness. Cook then discovered the ice island of South Georgia and the South Sandwich Islands but further search of this area revealed nothing. Eventually, when south of the Cape of Good Hope, their outward route was crossed and so the circumnavigation of the world was completed.

ASHORE IN ENGLAND

They arrived back in England on 29th July 1775 having been away for three years and eighteen days. In that time only four men had died and only one of them through sickness.

Furneaux, Captain of the *Adventure* had missed the planned meeting with the *Resolution* in New Zealand and had arrived back a year earlier.

Again, there was hardly any attempt to let the people of Britain know what had been going on. Cook was discharged from the *Resolution*, which was then considered unsafe for further action, and went home. He was presented to the King, promoted to post-captain and made a Fellow of the Royal Society for his fine work in preventing scurvy at sea.

Many in the Admiralty thought that Cook had done well. He was now forty-eight years of age and had spent thirty years, almost constantly, at sea. His health had broken down. During his last voyage he had suffered great pain from stomach ulcers, aggravated by the constant mental strain and stress. He was offered the captaincy of Greenwich Hospital, a well-paid job and one that would enable him to have time at home and some time was necessary for writing the account of his voyage and for arranging its publication. He took the position after much consideration.

NORTH-WEST PASSAGE

Cook had already solved one world problem when he discovered Australia. There was land in the Pacific Ocean — a lot of it. Another was solved when he proved that if there were land in the Antarctic region it would not be habitable on account of the fact that the ice did not disperse or melt during summer months. There was another problem that had been given much thought and action since the fifteenth century. It was whether it was possible to sail from the Pacific to the Atlantic Ocean by way of the North Pole. It was thought that salt water did not freeze. At this time, in spite of the observations made recently by Cook, scientists still hopefully held to the theory that, in the summer time, the ice would melt and disperse and leave a sea through which ships could sail. The Bering Strait had been found but whether a through passage could be negotiated was questioned by the authorities. The North-West Passage was a desirable theory because of the effect it would have on trade with Asia. It would be so much quicker for ships to go by way of the Pole than round the Cape of Good Hope.

The discovery of a north-west passage was so important to trade that in 1745 Parliament was persuaded to pass an act which offered a reward of $40,000 (£20,000) — a vast sum in those days — for its discovery.

The men of the Admiralty wanted Cook to take command of a third expedition to attempt a passage but they hesitated to ask him. He was a tired man and very far from well. However, they did keep in touch with him and asked him for his directions from time to time. They decided the best way to go about it would be to ask him who, he thought, would be the man to take command. They placed all the plans before him. He finally volunteered to accept the position himself, much to the satisfaction of the Admiralty.

Cook wrote nothing of his personal affairs in his journals. Beaglehole gives pertinent information when he says that Cook spent no time, emotion or energy on the opposite sex — except for his Elizabeth. From this we can get some feeling for what he had to go through to make this decision and to speak of it to one who had gone through so much anxiety for so long.

SAILING ORDERS

They were to sail around the Cape of Good Hope, stopping at Cape Town for stores. They were then to sail to Tahiti, calling in at New Zealand if Cook thought it necessary, restock and then sail to New Albion, as the west coast of

North America was then called. When sailing up that coast he had orders not to explore rivers or inlets until in the latitude 65° then he was to explore any inlet or river pointing in the direction of Hudson Bay or Baffin Bay. They were to arrive at latitude 65° by June 1777, look for a passage and, if one was found, sail through it and return to England. If they did not find one, they were to winter at Petropavlovsk, in Russia or some place they found that was better and try again in the spring of 1778.

SHODDY REFIT

It was Cook's idea that two ships would be best for the trip so it was decided, by the Admiralty, to refit the *Resolution* and to obtain the *Discovery* which was a new ship. Cook was to command the expedition on the *Resolution* and Captain Charles Clerke was to be in command of the *Discovery*.

Because of the delay in refitting the *Resolution,* the orders from the Admiralty were no longer practicable. To make matters worse, it was not long before it was found out that the refitting job had been badly done. Cook was not given time to supervise this work, as his time had been taken up working at the hospital, writing up reports, drawing new charts and trying to finish a book about his previous voyage. The poor refit could have been one of the factors contributing to his early death.

THIRD VOYAGE

Cook, of course, took the same precautions for the safety of his men as he had done on the previous expeditions and saw that the necessary food was loaded. There were 112 men on the *Resolution* and 70 on the *Discovery*. Many men had sailed with Cook before and some had been on both his voyages.

The intention was to leave at the end of April 1776 but it was not until 12th July that the *Resolution* left Plymouth. A week later the *Discovery* left. It was not many days before they found that the *Resolution* was leaking. They had to spend time at Table Bay having repairs carried out. This was Cook's fourth visit there and he was received with honours. The *Discovery* joined them at Table Bay and at the end of November they sailed for New Zealand. On the way the *Resolution* suffered damage to two of her masts.

They again met the *Discovery* this time at Queen Charlotte Sound, New Zealand, and they then sailed for Tonga, calling at several islands on the way. Then, after four weeks sailing, they arrived at Tahiti. By the time they got there, it was obvious that they could not keep to their schedule. The delays had made it impossible for them to be in the arctic region for the summer months and so they spent from August till December in Tahiti. One reason for the stay was that the food was plentiful and they would be able to stock up well when the fresh fruit and vegetables were available.

NEW DISCOVERIES

Enquiries were made as to whether there were any more islands to the north but no one knew of any so it was thought they would be having a long but clear time of sailing. They now had six months before they need be in the arctic region. Following instructions they headed for the west coast of North America, heading north in order to meet the westerlies, which in olden times, 'drove the galleons home'.

On December 24th, they came upon an uninhabited island which was promptly named Christmas Island. After several days, they sailed north-west and on 20th January Cook sighted more land. He had discovered the group of islands which are now known as the Hawaiian Islands. He discovered several islands and on 20th January he anchored off the island of Kauai.

The ships stayed there for nearly two weeks and during that time the natives seemed to sense that Cook was an exceptional man and they would fall to the ground in front of him. He only went ashore on three days during the fortnight. Good trade was done and food taken on board.

NORTH AMERICA

They were in plenty of time now to reach the arctic regions by June of 1778, so he thought, but he had not counted on two things. One was the need for repairs and the other gale force weather. They sailed up the particularly difficult coastline of what are now the states of Oregon and Washington naming many bays and headlands and, after braving the tests of one of the world's most vicious headlands, he named it Cape Flattery.

Many people living a purely social life, in which flattery, by look or word, plays such a leading role, could be completely unaware of what has happened to them as a result of depending on this practice. Here is a man who has had practically no social life at all giving the name Cape Flattery to the association of cliff and sea in a part of the world where the sea has the habit of sucking in the ships and sending brave men to the bottom in a very short time. What perfect insight into the way flattery sucks people in before they have time to realize it.

As they progressed he also determined the longitude of the

THE *ENDEAVOUR* AT SEA, by Sydney Parkinson

west coast of America. He found what is now Cook's Inlet — one of the very few of his many discoveries called after him. Again repairs were carried out and also time was spent exploring this river to see if by any chance it led to Hudson Bay. They anchored there at a point near where Anchorage now stands in Alaska. He then found a channel through the Aleutian Islands, gave their correct position, made the first recorded observation of the outflow of the mighty Yukon River and charted the coast of Alaska. They then made their way through the Bering Strait until they reached the northern tip of Alaska. Everything possible was done to penetrate the ice but to no avail.

ARCTIC REGION

Alan Villiers gives a vivid picture of the experiences that Cook and his men had at this time.

"Cook forced the reluctant Whitby collier right up to the ice, enormous impregnable fields of it, not far from Point Barrow. If a sea passage reached east towards the Atlantic past here — as indeed it did — he saw that it must be ice-jammed and useless, as indeed it was. He dodged the ships about between the rocky land and the great ice-fields, taking care not to be nipped. For the ice moves and the land is constant: a ship caught between would be ground to pieces. Cook extricated himself after a close look at the ice-field, the southern edge of which was some twelve feet high and the interior much higher — patient, impassive, endless, the last enemy in the North Pacific: but by no means silent. All along the edges it was noisy with the sea's surge; great floes ground together in the swell, lifting and smashing with a sort of malevolence which was frightening to watch and hear, as if the ice was grinding its massive teeth to get at the ships."

Cook then turned the expedition south charting a part of the Siberian coast and made for harbour in Unalaska. From here he sent dispatches to London.

As they were late and the height of summer had passed he decided to try again the following summer. He could have decided that they stayed passively on the Siberian coast at Petropavlovsk and this would probably have been the easier way to choose the right moment for making another attempt to penetrate the Bering Sea. However, his main reason (and this is taken from his own journals) for not choosing this port was his dislike of being inactive for at least six months.

Through the work of his biographers, it is clear, too, that his concern for his men would have influenced him to get them to a warmer climate with the possibility of better food, in spite of the fact that that would bring to him the strain caused by his deep concern for the Islanders. He believed that the Islanders were free of venereal disease that was prevalent amongst the sailors and knew that there was no way he could guard the health of the Islanders against what he called the "fatal disease".

It has also to be remembered that, all through the three voyages, he had to cope with the results of being compelled by regulation to issue grog to the crew. It was inevitable that there would be drunken brawls from time to time. The fact that almost everybody was being subjected to the constant intake of a substance that is so highly addictive meant that the situation would be critical if the supplies ran out. This would be just another source of concern for him.

However, he made the decision to sail south, back to the Hawaiian Islands, for the winter months with the intention of returning north earlier the next year.

HAWAIIAN ISLANDS

The first island they arrived at was Maui and they were greeted again by many natives. He thought that word of their last visit had got around the neighbouring islands. Some of the natives came aboard and one was an old man to whom the natives showed great respect. He was obviously their chief and it was learned later that he was their king. He had come on board to sum up the white men and especially their chief.

Four days later the main island of the group now known as

Hawaii was discovered and for more than two weeks they slowly sailed along the north coast of this island looking for a place to land in order to carry out repairs once again. As they sailed along the coast, natives brought them fresh fruit and vegetables. They arrived at Kealakekua Bay, took soundings and judged it safe to enter.

An amazing spectacle awaited them. Thousands of the Hawaiians in canoes and as many swimming like "great shoals of fish" surrounded the ship and swarmed aboard, giving them a tumultuous welcome.

'LONO'

The tall distinguished looking Captain was met by a young chief and a priest and was hailed as the return of their god *Lono*, who, they believed, would return in the form of a man. *Lono* was their god of peace, happiness and agriculture. Now, Cook was aware of a word that sounded like *Lono* which meant chief or king and, when the natives were falling to the ground in front of him, he thought that it was their way of greeting their chief.

There must have been something about Cook that made them think he was a king and, in a sense, they were right. He was not a king over people but he was a king over his own thoughts, feelings and actions.

A short time later he was to meet the old man who had boarded his ship on the first island. This time he was dressed in a fine cloak and helmet of feathers. He was none other than King Kalaniopu. He took off his King's robes and gave them to Cook with many other gifts. The priest had made sure that the natives gave of their produce to please *Lono* and his *demi-gods* but it did not take long for them to see how much the *demi-gods* ate. Therefore, it was a relief to the natives that they left after three weeks when the ship was considered seaworthy again.

LAST WORDS

The last words that Cook is known to have written were written as they left this island. They were, "So ended our voyage with a discovery, which, though the *last* seemed in so many respects to be the most important." These are strange words in view of the fact that a further year of voyaging to many new territories had been planned.

The two ships sailed north again to reach the Arctic by mid-summer and put the question about the North-West Passage beyond doubt. They had travelled for only four days when a tropical storm blew up and the *Resolution* was demasted. It is said that, had the refit of the ship been done in the way Cook would have had it done, then he would not have had to return to Hawaii. He thought twice about returning to Kealakekua Bay but it was the only thing to do.

CHANGE OF MOOD

This time there was no welcome. Doubts had grown in the minds of the Hawaiians. The *demi-gods* took too much and did not have the respect for them that *Lono* had. Also the legendary *Lono* had many wives. This man or god had none and quietly refused their offer to rectify the situation. There were many incidents while the repair work was being carried out. The Hawaiians were sullen and thieving from the two ships was prevalent. One day, the *Discovery's* cutter was stolen. Cook decided to make an effort to end the trouble and make the peace.

COOK'S DEATH

In full regalia with nine marines under Lieutenant Phillips' charge, Cook went ashore to see King Kalaniopu. He asked for the boat's return. It was 14th February 1779. When the king was told of the theft, he willingly agreed to accompany Cook to the *Resolution* as hostage. This was the custom and it had been followed when there had been prior acts of thieving. He walked with Cook to the beach, where a large and excited crowd had gathered. Several young chiefs joined the throng and they now picked up stones and others darted into their huts emerging with spears and wearing heavy coconut-fibre breast plates. As Cook and Phillips calmly pushed through the crowd, two warriors dragged their king away from them. A warrior with a stone in one hand and a dagger in the other confronted Cook who ordered him to lay down his weapons but the native prepared to throw the stone. Still wishing to avoid bloodshed, Cook fired a blank shot at the Hawaiian and the marines fired a round over the natives' heads. Cook then faced the excited warriors and they parted to let him through. He ordered a cease-fire and, without reloading his musket he made his way towards the boat.

The Hawaiians, after seeing the flash of muskets and no one falling, thought the guns to be harmless and rushed at Cook from behind.

The natives' awe of Cook was such that while he faced them they would do nothing to harm him but, when he turned to signal the boats to come in closer, the priest hit him with a club and he fell into the water and, as he lay dazed, he was stabbed many times.

They soon realized the muskets were far from harmless as the enraged sailors, now without the restraint of Cook's influence, fired volley after volley and within minutes the beach was cleared and the shocked and saddened men returned to the ship.

Back on board the men gathered and quietly waited for orders. The new commander of the expedition, who was expected to give orders for retaliation, said nothing.Their leader, the one who had, by his determination, saved them from sickness and who, by his competence, had saved them many times from death, was dead. They had confidently accompanied him into the unknown over the most dangerous parts of the oceans of the world. In the words of one of the surgeon's mates, David Samwell; ''He was our leading star, which at its setting left us involved in darkness and despair.''

CAPTAIN COOK'S BURIAL AT SEA

CHARLES CLERKE

Captain Charles Clerke had taken part in all three voyages. Having to take command in a state of shock and grief would have been hard for a robust and healthy man. Charles Clerke was slight in build and depleted in health — suffering from consumption — but his mind was undaunted and he had the strength to be true to Cook's intentions. Although he could not prevent the immediate retaliation that took place on the beach or minor skirmishes, he did prevent further counter attacks, in spite of the fact that James King, the loyal but not so level-headed second lieutenant, was, at first, strongly for retaliation.

Because of the customs of the natives, Cook's body was not given back for several days and then it was only his bones. On February 21st 1779, the remains of the body were, with full naval ceremony, sunk into the waters of the bay.

The next day the mast was raised and rigged and they departed. There was little wind and the progress was slow. Clerke, in continuing Cook's mission, returned to the Arctic and it was not until he was satisfied that there was no North-West Passage that he turned south. Soon after turning for home, Clerke died and was buried on the coast of Russia. He was only thirty-eight.

JOHN GORE

Lieutenant John Gore was the next to take command and the two little square riggers arrived back in England on 4th December, some eight months after the tragic event in the Pacific.

Gore took the vacancy at the Greenwich Hospital; the

ship's surgeon, Anderson had died at sea of consumption; Vancouver, Bligh, Burney and Grindall went on to become famous and most of the others went on to live their lives in obscurity. The men of the crew considered it an honour just to have their names recorded as having been on the voyage with such a man as Cook.

ENGLAND

At the news of Cook's death, the King wept. England had heard of Cook's death but not much about his life. There was nothing to tell about that North-West Passage; nor was there any $40,000 (£20,000) to distribute amongst the men. This third voyage was the longest — four years and three months. Cook's record was regarded as a miracle of the eighteenth century — three voyages taking over ten years at sea without a single life lost to scurvy. That they did survive must have been due both to the endurance capacity of the men and to their attitude to Cook.

ELIZABETH COOK

What of Elizabeth Cook? She was only thirty-eight years of age when her husband was killed. She had lost three children and three were surviving at the time of his death. However, in October 1780, one of them was lost at sea off the coast of North America. In December 1793, another son died from a violent fever. In January 1794, her eldest and only surviving child was robbed and killed when he was joining his naval ship. She did not recover from these experiences for many months.

To have been separated for so long from a husband who had such capacity for kindness and understanding and to know that his life was constantly in danger must have taken great toll of her health. Besides all this she was coping, during these years, with comparative poverty. That she survived to be ninety-three shows what great vitality and health she must have had to start with.

MRS. ELIZABETH COOK — artist unknown

Few men have borne the strains that Cook bore on account of the kind of difficulties he faced all the time. Some of the difficulties and responsibilities are not mentioned here and some may not be mentioned anywhere as he was a quiet, modest man not given to talking about his own feelings or deeper thoughts.

Few women have borne the strains that Elizabeth Cook bore on account of having lived through the death of such a husband and also through the deaths of all their six children and on account of her husband's mission, which, whatever else it was, was a very particular kind of service to humanity.

THE KING'S AWARD

King George 111 recognized the greatness of this life-work and posthumously awarded him a coat of arms. No one has since been given the same award by the reigning monarch for service to the nation. It is in blue and yellow and depicts the world. On it are two mottoes, one "Around the Globe" and the other, "He left nothing unattempted."

HUMAN QUALITIES

A story that tells of the way some man or woman has matched a great task with the appropriate human qualities is not only thrilling but strengthening.

Outstanding physical and mental vigour are not always associated with inborn tact, modesty, tolerance and respect for others but these qualities in Cook proved essential for contact with so many different native peoples and with others too.

Success and impressive appearance often bring about

arrogance and are not always associated with understanding for many different temperaments and backgrounds. This capacity was essential for the managing of such an explosive sort of situation with so many clashes of personality in such a small space and in such trying conditions for such long periods of time. Without tremendous self-control, the voyages could not have been managed in such a way that a reliable biographer could say that Cook was both loved and feared by his men. Many must have loved the man and feared the disapproval of the captain in him.

In him, calmness in personal danger had to be associated with the ability to become suddenly a picture of anger. In those who have little control, anger is an indulgence that can take the life out of others as well as wreck the health of the person allowing the anger to rise up and take control of him. In those who have exceptional control it is a sacrifice of health to the task of trying to get the job done properly or quickly enough. This sort of anger in one can put iron into the souls of others.

THE QUESTION

Discovery of the earth has now been performed. Man has, since then, made the earth, the air and the sea sick and has caused so much unnecessary suffering to many species of animals.

Could this be partly because, during this century, the adult population has failed to take an interest in the development of human qualities such as are seen — not, of course, in perfection but in active development — in James Cook? Readers may have other ideas about why so much damage has been done this century.

MODERN DISCOVERY

In the twentieth century we need to become discoverers in a different way and everyone can take part in the endeavour that leads to the discovery of the potential of man. The discovery can start with noticing that we are sometimes not as patient as we could be. A person who does not work at developing patience and perseverance (without talking about it but just doing it) cannot do anything but slide backwards and downwards. Discovery that is modern, basic and urgently needed therefore takes place in time and not in space. It takes time to develop the necessary qualities and, without developing them, we cannot really help to lessen the pollution of the earth, the air and the sea, as this outer pollution is only a reflection of the pollution of our minds. Why is it that we are so proud of making discoveries in outer space when we have done practically nothing about discovering what is going on in our thoughts and feelings? This sort of discovery has been important for a long time but now it is urgent.

OUR OPPORTUNITIES

From the studying of the lives of great people, we can get the stimulus to notice a thing or two about our own lives and some will have the energy to make improvements in themselves with as much interest as many now take in improving their houses.

James Cook has influenced our lives by discovering Australia and so leading the way for us to be able to live in this beautiful country.

If we can find the humility to accept this man's influence, his life can stimulate us to develop calmness, patience, presence of mind and everything else that would help us to become, in time, masters of our own souls.

This is the greatest adventure for these times and much depends on how many take it on and stick at it. It certainly requires many a strong resolution but it will lead to one interesting discovery after another and it does represent a truly modern endeavour.

CAPTAIN COOK'S STATUE, WHITBY, by John Tweed

77

PERSONS WHO LEFT ENGLAND IN H.M.S. ENDEAVOUR
26th AUGUST 1768

A date following the name signifies the date of death during the voyage.

J. Cook. Lieut. in Command

CREW

Z. Hicks. Lieut., 25.5.1771
J. Gore. Lieut.
R. Molineux. Master, 15.4.71
R. Pickersgill. Mast. Mate
C. Clerke. Mast. Mate
F. Wilkinson. A.B.
J. Bootie. Mid., 4.2.1771
J. Monkhouse. Mid., 6.2.1771
P. Saunders. Mid.,* 25.12.1770
I. Smith. A.B.
W. Harvey. Lieut's. Servant
J. Magra. A.B.
I. Manley. Mast. Serv.
W. B. Monkhouse. Surgeon, 5.11.70
W. Perry. Surgeons Mate
R. Orton. Clerk
S. Forwood. Gunner
J. Gathray. Bo'sun, 4.2.1771
J. Satterly. Carp., 12.2. 1771 ·
J. Thompson. Cook, 31.1.1771
S. Evans. Quartermaster
A. Weir. Quartermaster, 14.9.1768
T. Hardman. Bo'sun's Mate
J. Reading. Bo'sun's Mate, 29.8.69
B. Jordan. Carp.'s Mate, 31.1.1771
J. Ravenhill. Sailmaker, 27.1.1771
G. Nowell. A.B.
I. Parker. A.B.
R. Anderson. A.B.
J. Gray. A.B.
R. Taylor. Armourer, 1.8.1771
R. Hutchins. A.B.
J. Childs. A.B.
P. Flowers. A.B., 2.12.1768
T. Rearden. A.B., 24.12.1770

J. Ramsay, A.B.
W. Dawson. A.B.
F. Haite. A.B., 1.2.1771
S. Jones, A.B.
J. Nicholson, A.B., 31.1.1771
F. Sutherland. A.B., 30.4.1770
T.Simmonds, A.B.
R. Hughes. A.B.
S. Moody, A.B., 31.1.1771
I. Johnson, A.B.
R. Stainsby, A.B.
W. Collett, A.B.
A. Wolfe, A.B., 31.1.1771
M. Cox, A.B.
C. Williams, A.B.
A. Simpson, A.B. 21.2.1771
T. Knight, A.B.
H. Stevens. A.B.
T. Jones, A.B.
A. Ponto, A.B.
J. Dozey, A.B., 7.4.1771
J. Tunley, A.B.
M. Littleboy, A.B.
J. Goodjohn, A.B.
J. Woodworth, A.B., 24.12.1770
W. Peckover, A.B.
R. Littleboy, A.B.
H. Jeffs, A.B., 27.2.1771
W. Howson. Capt's Serv., 30.6.1771
N. Morey, Lieut's Serv.
T. Jones, Sur's. Serv.,** 5.11.1770
E. Terrell. Carp's Serv.
T. Jordan. Bo'sun's Serv.
T. Matthews. Cook's Serv.
D. Roberts. Gunner's Serv. 2.2.1771
J. Thurmand. A.B., 3.2.1771